BAD ALL OVER

J. ANDREW THOMAS

Also by J. Andrew Thomas

Suburban Purgatory Hell
Mauled by Death in the Hot Rain
Staring into the Void of Destruction
College is for Losers (Novel)
The Garden Gnomes are Watching
Sometimes You Get Lucky and the Problem Fixes Itself
Poems for Another Day
Cattle Prod (Novel)
All My Friends are on Television
Swallow God Swallow Nothing
With Pugs
The Bastards Will Always Win
Non-Union (Novel)
Ocean Currents (Play)
She Catches Her Breath in a Sob (Play)
The Greats are not so Great
A Place To Go When Things Went Wrong (Play)
Dead End Poems
Empire of Nothing (Novel)
Back to the Bars
Let Me Hold Your Heart Like a Flower (Play)
Dumb But Not Quite Damned
The Loud Thunderous Roar of Girls Searching For Invisible Love (Play)
It's Not Going to Get Better Only More Comfortable
Pitchfork (Novel)
Spring in Shamrock (Novel)
To Darkness Through a Wreath of Sudden Pain (Novel)
Wallowing in Obscurity
For a Second (Screenplay)
Nothing Doing Here There Anywhere
Bad Design
Her Candle so expire (Novel)
The Fat of the Day (Play)
Looking Down From Below

One Win Choice (Screenplay)
Spider in a Forest Fire
People Were Smaller Back Then (Play)
Super Busy Doing Absolutely Nothing
Three Porches (Play)
Sheep Drive
A Short Farewell (Play)
Hank and Emma and Sometimes Leo
We Should Not Expect Them to Be What We Want Them to Be
The Protected Wild (Novel)
To the Crowd (Short Stories)
See the World Burn
The Tail End of (play)
Time Again Later
Some Peace (play)
from a flowerless land
Says You (play)
Punching into Nowhere
A Perpetual Possibility (Novel)

BAD ALL OVER

no one has ever read this shit

it sits on every shelf
like some cool decoration
rather than a great work of
fiction

it pops out immediately to the eye

it is a great title...INFINITE JEST...

most normal people like myself
think

what the fuck does that mean?

why is it so big?

the author has three names, he must be
very smart!

and yes he was a highly intelligent man
and a nutjob
and a self important dick bag
but
that book
it sits on myself
reminding me of my early years
discovering literature
thinking I could read it if I gave myself enough time
and
now
it just weighs down my shelf
looking pretty and interesting
and I still have no idea what the fucking thing
is about.

it's coming soon

he's getting big
walking around
almost 2
and soon
he'll be at that stage
a little youngster
5-10 years old
the good years
where he will be sitting at the table
and I'll be serving him pancakes
on Sunday morning
like Joe Pesci in *Goodfellas*
with that big smile on his face
feeling like the best dad on the planet
and
how fucking great will that be!

it's bad bad bad

just
stay in your shell
don't look around
just
keep your head
in that shell
it's not good out there
just
keep in that shell
it's bad bad bad bad
just keep it in
like smart turtles
they know what they are doing
they know the way
they know how to get through life
just keep it in
keep the head in the shell
and
let life
happen
and you will be in darkness...

these days

everyone is a star
all you gotta do is hit an app
and you see normal no nothing people
doing amazing shit
and
nobody cares
nobody
nobody
they are so fucking talented!
and
nobody cares!
including me!
what the hell is wrong with us?
these people practiced for months….years…
and we watch 20 seconds and were like…ok
who fucking cares? I'm hungry and I need a drink
so
lets fucking go….!

a calm world

word
gone
so typing on this archaic notepad
thing
and
it's still word
and my hands are doing something
i had to do it
and it feels good
really good
it's been a while
and
i've been itching to get some
stupid shit down
so
here it is
are you entertained? no?
neither am I. but i do
like
typing
late night
when
they are all in bed
and it's just me
and it's calm..

like always

she keeps telling me to grow a beard but
I can't I can't I can't
I fucking can't because
I still look very young
like I'm 25 and if I change my look
I think I'm closer to death and
I'll jinx myself
and I just want to look the same my whole life
and hopefully I can last past 60
because
I have a son now
and a wife that loves me more than anything
and
if again
if I change my look
I will DIE. so let's just keep the clean face
like
ALWAYS.

he watches

as I go back and forth
with the lawn cutting machine
I look right
toward the house
and there he is
at the window
SMILING
as cute as I've ever seen him
he's so fucking awesome
almost 2
and
he sees his old man
mowing
and all I can think about that line from
Jerry Seinfeld talking about how
parenting advice
saying
kids will never take any kind of advice you give them
but
if you set a good example
if you just be a good person
if you do some hard shit
the good example
if you just be a good person
if you do some hard shit
they will subconsciously
take after you
and
do what you do
and all I can think about is
how similar I am to my dad
fixing shit
having old cars
mowing my grass
watching sports

eating bad food

and I'm so happy that little Eli
will
be like his dad

he won't be like these rich fucker kids
around this neighborhood
who
look out the window
and see
some weird guy
mowing their grass

as they sit in the easy air conditioning

no
my boy
will
do shit on his own
he will

fuck some shit up.

1 out of 3

"the manager called me before work…so annoying!"

"why?" I asked.

"he was telling me the schedule and asked me who I wanted
to work with. he gave me three names. Gil, Ed and you."

"oh yeah?"

"yeah, so obviously I chose you. Gil we would be here all day!"

"and Ed, Ed's a nice guy but he says some weird shit."

"I know! he's pretty good at his job but the stuff that comes out
of his
mouth…good lord I can't take that all day."

and for the first time in a long time
I felt a little good about myself. I beat out two
idiots
two incorrigible people
that nobody really liked

which really wasn't anything to crow about

but
it was better than nothing.

like I did

all these books on my shelf
were once for my wife to read
after I died
so she could have some piece of me
because I'm pretty sure she's living to 90
and
there's no way I'm getting there
but
now that I think about it
they might be for Eli as well
when he gets to that age
where you think you can make it
outside of the rat race
where you look at all the millionaire artists
and writers and actors and all the other
lucky bastards
and you want to do that
rather than
be chained to a horrible job the rest of your life…

I'll show him all these books I've written and
how nobody gives a damn
telling him I had big dreams of being a published writer
who could pay my bills with my words
and the only way I was able to afford
giving him a good life in this big house
eating good food
driving nice cars
watching giant TV's on all floors of the house
playing awesome video games
turning down the air conditioning as low as we want
to be as comfortable as we want

it all came from trudging into the stupid fucking job
every god damn day for my whole life

not giving into the fantasy
of sitting in my office and typing away
hoping somebody will put my shit out there
and pay me

no
fuck that
don't rely on them. rely on yourself.

and then
he will roll his eyes and not listen at all
and do his own thing
but
all I can say is

"I tried" and then
hopefully
he will make mistakes and learn from them
and
get where he needs to be

like I did.

just the sight

the small black spider
crawls up the giant white wall
and
he's minding his own business
out from the shadows
he decides to make a move to
another part of the house
and continue
hiding
and eating invasive insects that enter
the peoples home
helping them out
without them even knowing
and
then
he's spotted
and
just the sight of him
MINDING HIS OWN BUSINESS
is horrifying
a paper towel is
grabbed
and
a few seconds later
he's going down the toilet.

I'm back

at the keyboard
after a few weeks of
bullshit
and
it feels good
like
a*this is where I belong*
kind of thing
and
it only took
40 years to figure it out…

think back

10 years

all that stupid shit

that ruled your life
that mattered most
that made you sick
that you worked your ass for

and now

it seems meaningless

and
it's so disturbing
that
what rules your life now

won't matter much to you

20 years from now

you won't give a fuck
and you will probably brow beat yourself for
being so stupid
for caring about the dumb bullshit

and
then
then

we die

and
nothing will matter

which is what God wants…

This American Life

Generations from now
I'm talking 200 years or so
the "people" if that's what they still call
themselves
will look back
at how we lived
us Americans
and they will very confused at how we fell
at how we had everything we could ever want
unlimited resources and food and money and
EVERYFUCKINGTHINGYOUCANTHINKOF
and we didn't care, it was too much, we were too happy and that
made us too sad to keep it all going…we focused on the hate
and we spewed horrible shit at each other everydayand then it
ended like every other
empire in the history of the world…ours…we thought would last
forever
and as I write this, I still can't believe we will fall one day and this
kind of life will be gone forever and hopefully I'll be ashes by the
time
that happens…

a few lanes down

as I let the young high school guy scan my grocery card
I saw her a few lanes down
the hot skinny goth girl with the piercings and the bored look
on her face...

I was immediately transported back to McDonald's
working as a 15 year old...

fuck
            fuck
                fuck

all I thought of was if I worked there
I would be tortured
thinking of ways to make this girl
think I was cool and to date me...

and at the end of the day
the end of the year working there
I would never say one word to her...

which was probably for the best
now that I look back

because
there was no way I could have made that
kind of woman happy

no
fucking
way...

the things have changed

dog tired this morning
feeling like shit
wishing I went to bed earlier
the night before
and
here I am again
approaching that god damn midnight
and
I want to keep going
because it's so quiet in the house
and
nobody will bother me
I can finally write this stupid bullshit!

is it worth it?

stay up until 1am?
which used to be nothing
when I was on the night shift

4 or 5 was the standard

but
now it's one a fucking m.

maybe 12:30
split the difference. and
hope
if I drink a shit load of water
I'll be ok

and
sleep until 8am…

the gamblers way

you bet
and
you
lost
and then you bet again
double
and
then you got back to even
which
is the real
win
because
you can
wake up
hungover
and
get drunk and
bet
tomorrow.

no one is safe

you write long enough
you will start to repeat yourself

even the most talented and
accomplished writer
can't avoid this.

that's just the way it is.

just the way it is.

qualifications to run for United States President

as I look at the dirty mentally deranged
bums on the city streets
looking for money and drugs and drink...

all I can think about is

they could run for President if they want

there's literally no qualifications
to be the most powerful man on the planet right now...
none...just be the age of 35 and born in the US and been
living here for 14 years...that's it...you can be a god damn
criminal
and you can still run this great country...

how fucked up is that?

even O.J. can make a run if he wants...

Paul Hockman

he was a good man who grew up
in the mid 20th century on a farm learning the ways
of the land
and
life was always simple for him
which is the way he liked it
and never drank or smoked and he always went to
church and loved his family more than
anything in life
and was
a great dad and now he's gone
and
they don't make them like him anymore
which is a
damn shame.

it's so fucking easy

you turn on your phone
hit a button
and
someone is getting brutally murdered with a
meat cleaver

blood everywhere

and
I'm completely unaffected
it's
like I'm watching a movie
it doesn't affect me at all
like
it's not real

....but it is. it's very very very real
and

 they want us
not caring about anything
and
eventually
when
they pull your neighbor out of their house
and shoot him dead
because he had the wrong "opinion"
like
Orwell predicted...it's coming and there's nothing we
can do about it
so
I'll just sit here and write and drink and watch
lovely movies and TV and
wait for the end
and when it comes

I'll smile…I'll smile and know that I we had a good run.

another one

"he said he gave up drinking because
he went on some
program for 90 days and he feels better
than ever so he never went back.."

blah
blah
blah
blah

again and again and again

it's always the same

yes
yes
yes

we know!

we all feel great not drinking!

it's amazing!

waking up feeling energized and not hungover!

but
but
but

what about the high? the click you get? when you hit the right
amout
of booze?

you hear that one song and your life finally has meaning?

and
now
you have nothing. you eat. you watch TV. that's it. you
don't get out of your mind at all. which is a damn fucking shame.

GET OUT. IT'S BAD IN THERE! life is fucking boring unless
you are a
millionaire and they are bored too if they are sober…TRUST ME.
THEY RUN
THROUGH SO MANY YOUNG GIRLS IF THEY CAN'T GET
FUCKED UP.

it's always something..

big and fat and rich

what should I do?

dedicate my life to making money
give up on everything else
and
just eat and get rich and look horrible
but be really happy
on a boat
giving the middle finger to everything and everybody?

or
keep doing what I'm doing
not giving a fuck about
anything or anybody
just working and living paycheck to paycheck
writing
and eating just to get by
driving my shit car
loving my wife and my child
never even thinking about having a vacation home
just happy to be alive
drinking cheap beer from a can
like I'm back in college…

yeah…yeah…the latter…

garbage taste

these fuckers
who
all grew up poor
now
they can't eat shit food
because they are rich

they still love the terrible food
the easy
fried bad awfulness

the garbage taste

these fuckers
who
all grew up poor
now
they can't eat shit food
because they are rich

they still love the terrible food
the easy
fried bad awfulness

they LOVE IT!

THEY FUCKING LOVE IT!

like me
I have garbage taste in food

I don't care about food
I want to write and booze and
jerk off and play video games and
watch old movies

take the food
take it

you eat it in 30 seconds and it's gone
so
what?

I'll do some other shit

why not
right?

give it up

the world has been always ending
since
civilization started
we all think
humanity is terrible and there's no way
we can keep going on
forever
but
now
now
it's not looking good
yes
I'm one of those people
the ice is melting
and
the scientists
are worried
the smart fuckers
they know
they know
they know
so
it might happen
not when I'm alive
but
in 50 years
but
god
then what?
all that shit we created?
all those great movies and books
what happens?
it all goes away forever
lost
lost

lost
lost
forever
even Moby Dick
is
gone forever
so
why the fuck am I still writing?

walking by

you've passed them
many times
and their face is as familiar
as your spouse
and
here we go again
they are coming towards me
and
I almost want to say "hello"
but
then
I think
damn
what about tomorrow?
and the day after?
and the day after that?
you've always walked by with your head
down and it's been so easy to say nothing
even though
you feel like you should and for a moment
after they've passed
you feel bad
but
what's the alternative? a smile and hello
every god damn fucking day?
NO
NO
NO
I can't handle that!
and
then
the moment arrives and you
keep your head at a 45 degree angle
not down or up
but

in the middle
thinking
ok, fine, I'll do it
and they have their head down
thinking
this is what we do
so
even try to make eye contact with this
antisocial fuck.

and then there's that few seconds
after
both of us
walking away from each other
and
I feel like total shit
like I'm better than you and
you don't deserve to even look at
me...

which is the exact opposite of how I feel.

you hate

what they've become

it's a complete 180 degrees from
their younger self
who created all that great shit
that you loved and still watch
which takes you back to your youth
when the world seemed so much better
but
even though you don't relate to them
in their present evolved state
whatsoever anymore
you can't be mad at them. everyone dies
slowly
everyone gives up eventually
this is their way of dealing with life now
and who fucking cares. they had it for a while
and now they don't.
you can still watch that old shit
over and over and over and it doesn't get
tiring. it's perfect.

unlike most things in life.

just to give you an update

they start out saying
in a post
and they drone on about what they are up to
and what's coming up next
content wise
and then they trumpet how amazing it's been
being off social media
and now life is so much better not tied to
looking at posts all day
but they will eventually be back when
"life calms down"
because they are dealing with some real shit
and
all the while
I'm thinking
YOU ARE POSTING THIS ON SOCIAL MEDIA
IF IT'S SO TERRIBLE WHY ARE YOU BACK? WHY
DIDN'T YOU DELETE EVERYTHING AND LIVE
YOUR LIFE…IF IT'S SO GREAT?
and there's a condescending tone to all of it
it's like
yeah, I got clean and here you are
you idiots, you weak fuckers
on twitter
mindlessly scrolling your life away and I'm
out and here's a quick update on my life
ON SOCIAL MEDIA
the thing I just said I hate now and it's the devil
and
I just scroll past and shake my head
not really caring because
in 2 seconds there's some other crazy shit being said
by some lunatic and it's all marvelous
marvelous, marvelous this inner dialogue
all out there

for everyone to see
and somebody is going to get fired tomorrow for
something they said
and
all I can do is watch and laugh.

hadn't had a drink in...

and there's that phrase
while looking up some Hollywood actor
I admire
and there's some reason they stopped
like they had some injury or sickness or just got
plain tired of the booze
and then
I look up their age
hoping they made it past 50 and then
I do some math
and
it's usually late 40's, early 50's and I feel a sense
of relief
knowing I have a few more years
until I need to make a big
decision.

they are enlightened now

WHAT THE FUCK? HOW CAN THEY
FUCKING SAY THAT? WHAT A FUCKING
HYPOCRITE! I USED TO LIKE THEM AND NOW
THEY ARE ACTING LIKE THEY ARE BETTER THAN
ALL OF US BECAUSE THEY "SAW THE LIGHT"

and you want to say some crazy shit
on social media about them
trying to get them cancelled for their past
insensitive jokes about everybody and everything
and that's what made them famous
because they didn't care what people thought about them
but
now
they are grown up with a family and kids
and the Hollywood money is coming in
so
they have to denounce all that past shit
you are enraged
the more and more you read about how they've
grown and everyone else who hasn't grown with them
should stay cancelled because they are
like cavemen who still make those "kind" of jokes
and then
you look at your life and it's going great
it's peaceful and nobody bothers you and
if you keep going on this path
nothing will go that wrong unless it's some
awful freak accident that can happen to anybody
so
you decide
to take a breath and
think about it for a second…you won't have to say a thing
there are a million other nutjobs out there with nothing
to lose

who think the exact same way you do
and they will say all that nutty shit
online
they will talk for you
and
all you gotta do is sit back and read and
laugh
and continue on with this easy
existence.

the other half of the world

is turning to WAR
it's total chaos
people saying it's going to turn into WW3
and
it's all on tape now
all on video
we are seeing every fucking thing
shit
we shouldn't see
bombings
shootings
tanks running over cars
and it's just the start
someone at work said
"imagine if they had phones back in WW2"
and
the thought of that…
you want to think if we were watching videos of
people getting gassed and burned alive
in those horrible camps
we would stop living our lives and do something
about it
but no
no
I don't think it would keep us from doing
everything we are doing now
watching these atrocities
lesser than
genocide, yes, but it's still fucking insane
watching innocent people dying
for
just living their lives…and tomorrow
well go do some fun shit here
with my family
like

nothing is happening
and
well feel bad for those people in Ukraine
but
what can I do?

the great American smokeout

she's gone one night
for work
and
have the house to myself
and
there's only one thing to do
buy a pack of smokes
and it feels like I'm buying drugs
like
I'm breaking the law
it's been so fucking long
but
I need to do it
because all I do is think about
lighting up
everyfuckingdayofmylife
and it won't ever stop
but
I have
one night to get it all out
so
I machine gun them
everyhalfhourlikeagoddamnmotherfuckinggangster
degenerateloster

and it's awesome and terrible all at the same time
and
by the time I'm at the last one of the night I'm ready
to throw up and I'm so glad I won't one of these
for a very long time
but
still
will think about it
everyfuckingdayofmylifeuntilIdie.
and

that's what they WANT.

meaningless like everything else

looking back at how we acted
years ago
many many many years ago
we are embarrassed at our stupid
brutish behavior
and
can't believe we did what we did
but
now
what are you doing? probably acting stupid
and foolish
why though?
why?
because the present is all that matters and
we won't understand how it all shakes out
and affect other people
until
a long time from now
and
well look back and go
what the fuck! why? none of it mattered!
it was all stupid and meaningless! why
did we think it meant so much!
it didn't!
and
then well die and we will be forgotten
and then and only then will it be
proven that most everything we've done in life
will not have mattered
one
fucking
bit.

all I got now

I see him walking around
smiling, smiling, sthe miling
like everything in the world is
grand

BECAUSE IT IS!

he's more loved than anyone
in the world right now

and then
a wave of black depression and
debilitating misery

hits me like a hurricane...

I start to think about him having to go out into the world

and deal with all the bullshit of other people...

he has no idea what he's in for. he's so naïve
like every other kid

will he be able to fit in? to assimilate with the
crowd?

or will he be like me? will he hate every minute
of school and his classmates...

                      ...wishing he was back at
home, never able to enjoy anything that involved those maniac
bullies who made life utterly intolerable...

hopefully I can prevent it from happening again…I have much
wisdom now…he's protected…nobody will fuck with this
kid…it's my main mission now…a few years to toughen him
up…he's all I got now…

out of nowhere

you turn the corner
and
there she is

BOOM!

like a surprise shotgun to the face

you say to yourself "woah"

it's
an unknown
woman or man

a stranger you've never seen before

it's
somebody who you would desire
if you saw them out at a bar

someone who is similar in physical attributes

someone who when you stand next to each
other

people would go…"they look like a nice couple"

and
they see you

the same

and then as you walk toward each other

not knowing what kind of look to give

as you walk by

you feel a stress, a tightness come over you
and you quickly decide

it's not worth it

and

you look down as your paths cross

which feels cowardly at the time
but
10 seconds later
and
50 more feet apart
you are glad
you didn't make eye contact

it's just easier that way. just keep going about
your day

it's all fake. nobody is real. life is bullshit.

don't get into trouble.

nothing good
can come of looking at the opposite
sex like that…

nothing…

I'll be back

the fight is over
the keyboard has won
took me down
I gave it my all
but now
I'm throwing in the towel
not much else to say
at this point
maybe I'll make a comeback
like Foreman in his 40's
we all love that
shit
need to go out and live some more
life
get some dumb shit to write about
get the brain working again
and then
I'll come back
fuck these keys up again
while
drinking 10,000 beers
so
well see
I don't think I can stay away forever
...thankfully....

it's all a trade off

everything in life
that is

all of it

you never get anything
without giving up something

unless
you are uber rich
and
then
you get it all

ALL
ALL
ALL OF IT
WITHOUT GIVING AN INCH

but us poor fucks
like myself
who has to work
everyday

me
yes
me

who currently works Tues-Sat

who
loves his Sunday nights
late night
alone
getting drunk

he's going to lose it soon
and
he will have to go to bed at an earlier time
to get up
Monday morning soon
so he can sleep in Saturday mornings…

that's the fucking trade off…

and he thinks…only if work weeks could start on
Tues…

not gay

yea well

there's something about a good looking man
who doing some cool shit
being creative
and not just fucking hot chicks

you can respect that shit
and you are jealous as hell

because they have it all
and
you will never get there

those damn arms and abs...fuck them!

and here I am
watching the music videos over and over and over
and over...

apes, all of us

it's no wonder
us men
us cave men
us mongrels
us animals
us fucking apes
the scum of the earth
who can lift heavy shit and jack off and
watch football for 8 hours a day

it's no wonder
we turn into insane serial predators when
when a good looking woman
comes within 3 feet of us

it's because after college
all these girls we used to see
every fucking day
every fucking class
every fucking walk outside

they leave! they graduate college and they
spread all over

out into the world
and

it's only every once in a while
we see one

and then
like I said before

we turn into fucking werewolves
who

can't control ourselves and need to be put down
by a silver bullet...

so just relax
ignore the idiots
who can't help
hitting you 24/7
they
can't help themselves

and just like in college
and in high school

I'll be in the background
trying to hide
from everyone...

not wanting to be apart of anything...

me, here, everywhere

if I could clone myself
like that Michael Keaton movie
Multiplicity

I wouldn't do it like he did
doing all this dumb bullshit

trying to keep up with house stuff
and wife stuff and work stuff...

no...

it would be all about TV and movies and video games...

all I can think about all day
is how much shit I want to watch
all the time
and

yet

I only have 2 eyes and one body and one life
and
so much free time...

oh my clones...god you would be so lazy...
you would be so entertained...

watching old 80's movies

dumb comedies

awful horror movies

damn dumb independent films

cult classics

war movies

early 90's sitcoms

cartoons...oh the cartoons!

god what could be!!

looks nice but I'll pass

they are on vacation
and
yet
they look they are at home
in their fancy houses...

now
that's
real
wealth...

a lifestyle I'll never
see
or can
even imagine...and I'm ok with it

because

behind that picture

it's all

bad, bad, bad....

(the money comes at a price and the family always
suffers)

Tuesday's Gone

comes on
and
it's a beautiful song…

there's nothing like it

I feel like I'm in *Dazed and Confused*
or
Happy Gilmore

not
my life

and
it's a good 7 minutes or so…

and I'm always amazed why
it's never played
on
the radio

what a travesty…

end of an era

"lets go out to the old smallmouth spot," I said to Ralph over the
phone.

it had been years since we went fishing
together

back in high school we practically went
every fucking day

the world was horrible for us back then and
we hated everything and everyone
except fishing

it kept us going when we didn't want to

and then
the years went by and
I could count the number of times
we wet some hook

"what, today?" he said.

"yea, you can still fish there. when's the last time
you been there?"

"long time. I got a boat now so no reason."

"oh, It's still good. I caught five last time. what time
you getting home?"

"nah, I don't think I'm going to go. by the time
I get home it's like 630 and I have to walk the dog
so it's a pain…"

"gotcha…"

and then I'm at the spot alone
casting my line out into the creek
and instead of enjoying nature
I'm
thinking about the old days
20 years ago

thinking about

how poor we were
how desperate we were to get laid for the first time
how depressed we were
hoping that in 10 years
we wouldn't have any of the problems we had then
we would older and have good jobs and hot chick girlfriends
and everything would be fucking awesome…

and if it didn't happen in 10 years
we would move the fuck away from this hillbilly town and
make it happen somewhere else.

and now
almost 25 years later
we're both still here
living 2 minutes away from each other

and we only see each other twice a year

things have changed
life is better in ways, worse in some
but
we are still here
good health
big bank accounts
comfortable amenities
and

best of all
we don't give a fuck what people think anymore

no

those days are gone forever
and
when I think about how much that fucked us up

always wishing we were popular
always wishing we had girlfriends
always wishing we were at a party instead of
fishing at some farm pond on a Friday night

and the toll it took on our
general outlook on life…

and now
us living 2 minutes down the street from each other
living totally separate and different lives
too busy to see each other
for a few hours…

bad all over

woke up feeling good today
like
the world is an ok place to live
and
the future will be bright
then
reading the news of the day
it says the Amazon rain forest
is being destroyed
faster than ever
the scientists call it the "lungs of the planet"
and say we are doomed if they
bastards continue at this rate
and
now I have to walk through the rest of the day
not caring about anything
knowing we have no shot at anything
the future will be bad
bad all over
way worse than anything you see now
now
it's nothing compared to the hell that is in
store for humanity
and
hopefully I'll be long gone before any of that shit
happens.

the world is an insane place to live
everyone thinks they are right all the time
woman never seem happy unless they are complaining
it's summer now and people should be happy but they aren't
I tell myself I'm going to go fishing this week
but it's almost 100 degrees out
air conditioning is the greatest invention in the history of man
no one can tell me different
everyone is angry out there. I sit home and watch TV
with my wife where it's safe.
out there, the nation is falling right in front of our eyes
nobody cares
as long as we got our high speed internet
our reality shows
our fast food
our unlimited supply of bullshit
that's all we need. pull a seat up. lets
watch together on our big leather couches
in the cold cold air conditioning
which by the way
is the greatest invention in the history of the world.

and again

at the keyboard
late at night
with the drink
and books above
wondering how long I'm going to last in the world
or
how long I'll outlast this stupid world
knowing
none of this shit doesn't even matter
which
makes me happy.

these kids

you hear about how you need to give them encouragement
to keep them going, to keep them happy, to keep them from
giving up
entirely
and I get it, I really do, kids are fragile, not much more than
adults but they
are
and we need to tell them they are doing a good job at whatever
they are doing if they
are indeed doing a good job

and then I look at all these adults I work with
these broken nutjobs
who have given up on life
who really need some encouragement
who need some nice words once in a while
and I wonder
what the fuck happened? why did we stop telling people they are
doing a good job
and
would it even matter to these fucks?
giving them something nice to hear?
or
do they just care about money now?

I'm not sure anything can fix them. they are too far gone.
no amount of money or "nice words" would do anything for
them...

stop over analyzing everything

we spend our lives
trying to make sense of this life on earth
this human life
and we don't get very far
no one who has ever lived has come up with the one and only
explanation
nope
no one ever. just theories that only some people will believe.
all I know is none of this shit doesn't make any sense.

and that's good enough for me. just give me a drink and a smoke
and I'm happy.

problems

she love me more than anything
and hates my mother
so
what the hell is this man supposed to do?

just drink and gamble and jerk off
like
I've always done…right?

it's all a man can do
plus
play video games and read and write
plays and novels and short stories
until
I'm in the ground…and then

nothing to worry about…

50 years later

our time
this time
the fucking present
seems so important to us
BECAUSE IT IS!
right?
it's our lives being affected right now...

.................but then...........in 50 years
our grandkids will look back
and scoff at how stupid we were
at how
ridiculous our lives were and how primal our thinking was
and
laugh
laugh
laugh
at how stupid we were and they will wonder

why did it matter so much to them?

and here we are
thinking
this is life or death...all this stupid shit we are worried about...life
or death...

fucking bullshit. all of it. yet, it won't ever stop. even the
grandkids will
think the same way...

an easy poet

is
me
I never wanted to be an intelligent person
never
ever
ever
no
or a rich man or an important man
no
never
ever
ever
no
just a good man
that's all I ever cared about
when I die
they will say he did his best
with what he had
and
that's all I can hope for

history might look upon the great geniuses
with fondness even though they were mostly
scumbags
and
horrible people
but
I don't give a fuck about that
just
be good
be nice
be a decent human fucking being
and don't cause distress
and
mind your own business

and
don't prey on young girls
which
all the geniuses do
don't they?

the sex
and the violence

that's the MO
they can't help themselves…not me
I just stay alone
writing and boozing and playing video games and
reading and watching movies and fucking my
wife

that's my MO. that's ok…right?

fuck the president

the president of this stupid United States
fell off his bicycle today
the 80 year old fuck
who should be in some Alzheimer home
just fell over
and looked like a complete idiot
for all the world to see on video
and
it's hilarious seeing everyone laugh at him
because
even though I feel bad for him because he's
out of his mind
and it's not his fault his brain is gone
he was once a younger man
a younger politician and he took advantage of the system
and fucked many many people who got in his way
it's just the way it is
to get to the top
you gotta be a heartless fucking bastard and now
he seems so innocent but fuck him
and
it's summer. summer everything is so much more fun.
seeing all the memes…it's so fucking fun…

fuck the president. he knows what he did.

don't hide behind this old man persona.

we know.

modern poetry

we read the old books and poems and all that shit
and it's so romantic
how they had absolutely nothing and people would actually
read books before bed because there was no TV, no internet, no
nothing
and words actually mattered…not these stupid opinions on social
media now
they don't matter at all, none of it, it's all fucking non-sense, no
those words in print in fucking books
they mattered
back in the day
and
we want to be able to write like but we can't. we will never be as
good as them
the old writers…they will always rule because they lived when
writing the most important thing in the world and
they will never die

as for these poems

just throw them in the toilet. they aren't worth a damn.

a simple man

the little midget man
my own half DNA
scratches the shit out of me
like a god damn wolverine
and
all I want him to is to go to sleep
but
he has other plans
I know he's tired but
he fights and fights
and eventually he gives in
poor little guy
and then everything is peaceful

one more of these little humans? I think…

how?

how do people juggle all these kids?

one is good for me. so simple.

I love simple.

my time

so angry as a young man
holy fuck
I don't like to think about it
and it all predicated on women
that's all men want
and that's whole problem with the world
we all want them
and when we can't get them
jesus
some crazy fucks will cause terror because they just want to get a
nut off
and
I can understand it
but
God damn I never came close to it
except the fantasy in my mind of turning my car into a semi
coming
at me
on the road because I was so angry and miserable
being constantly rejected…and luckily I rode it out
and
now
things are better than ever…but who knows if it kept going a few
more years
being alone and horribly depressed…fuck that.

here and not going back ever

this age...over 40...kid and a wife...the job...nice house...easy
life...nothing going on...I'm back to being a kid again...life is
great and I'm the happiest for the first time in a long fucking
time...I wear the matching shirt with my son that I got from my
wife on fathers day...never would have done that if I was in my
20's...but now I don't care...they don't tell you that when you
are younger...that you will stop caring and look like a complete
idiot...not caring one fucking bit...but here I am...out fishing on
fathers day with my kid wearing matching fucking shirts looking
like insane dorks...and it's wonderful not giving a fucking fuck
about anything...the one good thing about getting old...oh and
having more money...that too.

everyone is asleep

the world is dead
and
it's so peaceful
I still can't believe
people go to sleep so early
all the time
when you could be
up
and
awake
and
have distractions…

but
that would take
everyone going to sleep
so

yes
everyone
go to bed

let me play

let me
be alone

it's GLORIOUS. I am happy
you
are
not around

stay
where you are!

cave drawings

the stack of Playboy's and Penthouses
sat out in plain view
in the cardboard box
in my father's garage
and I glanced down and remembered seeing them
25 years ago

the same ones!

still in that garage!

and
instead of being filled with an excitement
I couldn't even begin to describe on paper

I strolled by and felt a second of nostalgia
followed by absolutely nothing…

and all I thought was

what a stupid time we used to live in!

these stupid magazines
actually made us idiot horny men
happy!

it's like we were cavemen
grunting and beating off to these simple
paper images

compared to how much content is
available nowdays…

which is probably way too much and it's going to lead to
more and more depravity

pulling us actually into the computer with fake robots
pretending to love us

and that will be the end of humanity

which is probably for the best...

this is it for now

the brain
is like glue now
it's like
I stopped caring about everything
except the baby boy and the wife
it's the most important thing in my life now
the family
like every other blue collar slob
in the existence of this country
and
that's how it's got to be for now
sooner
or
later
maybe
the words will come back
they come and go
here and there
but
nothing is retained
nothing seems important

nothing

just
food
money
milk
baby food
TV
cleaning

all that mundane shit
is
all that matters

but

soon
or
later
or
never

they will come back
and
I'll write some good shit

not this
complaining
awful
poems
that
I write
because I have
nothing
else.

it's yours right now

tired
but not drunk
and
it's a fight to get there, to the place you want to be
so
just write and keep pulling it in and in an hour
you will be there, to the promised land…it's the weekend
god fucking damn it…you got here and enjoy it…

poems >internet

you go online
and
it's the end of the world
it's total chaos
it's everyone shitting on everyone
and
you want to kill yourself
after reading
the inter monologue of
random people
for an hour
and
then
you go out
into the world
and
people
kind of keep to themselves and they
don't care about what you think
because
they can't read your thoughts
so
it's nice and peaceful…

so
maybe
lets
shut the internet
down…right?

2 hours in the office

is all I need

funny
how
I wish for all this dumb free time
to myself

and
then
I get it
and
I'm
like some stupid zoo animal who wants to
escape
so
so
so
bad
and then finally
after many attempts
he
gets out and then
he looks around at his strange environment
and goes
"oh, shit, what the fuck do I do? I'm lost!'

and
that's me
when
I have too much time to myself

I have no idea what the fuck to do
because I have
too many things I want
so

I get paralyzed
so
I just write poems and watch monkey and cat videos and
drink
and listen to music
which isn't bad
per se
but
it is a dumb time to spend
alone
when I could be doing
so much more.

they don't tell you

starting writing
and
stopping writing

both come
from the same place

and

they

might be the two
easiest things

in the entire world.

observing them in their natural environment
like a wildlife photographer

alone at a bar
watching strangers
they talk talk talk it all away
and it's all meaningless and stupid
and
all I do is write it down
back and forth to myself
and
I wonder who it's more satisfying to?
I guess
both of us
because we are doing what comes natural to us.

h a r d
t o
k e e p
i t
u p

were only young for so long
and
then
it gets fucking hard
nobody tells us
how
fat and ugly we will get
oh
wait
they do
they tell us
the horrible looking adults who are depressed and drunk
and high
and sad
they tell us
they say how we will fall
and
we can't believe it
we say it wont happen
and
watching this Smashing Pumpkins video
this
gorgeous bassist
who I used to love

well
she's a fat crazy broad now
who lives on a farm and can't play
anymore

and

I'm sadder and drunker than ever
because I'm an
adult.

one day, hopefully not

the kid shot baskets
in the middle of the road
wireless ear buds in there
no idea
if cars were coming
who the fuck knows where the parents were
everyday with this poor kid
nobody telling him
YOU GOTTA KEEP AND EAR OUT FOR FUCKING CARS!
NOT
EVERYONE IS AS NICE AS ME!
but he lives in a nice house with a nice family and
in this neighborhood nothing happens
so
he thinks EVERYTHING IS FINE and
it might not be
someday…

the end is neigh

"so what do you think? World War 3 coming soon?"

I said to the old woman who was wiping down the counters
at work.

"what?"

she waved her hand and groaned.

"I don't know, I don't even have a place to eat
my lunch...this place..."

"they keep bringing people in and cramming us
all together with no plan on where we should sit,
it's ridiculous," I said.

"nobody knows what they are doing here."

and she kept on with her job
taking out the trash, wiping down the counters
moping the floor
and
didn't seem to concerned about nuclear war
ending humanity
and
I couldn't blame her. she was right.
the break room space
seemed more important than any of that

why worry about something you can't control?

just focus on what's in front of you
everything else

is bullshit.

My Eli

I know the truth
he doesn't
because he's a baby
but
one day
he will know
the fucking horrible truth
that
santa Claus doesn't exist and
the Earth is doomed
but
for now
he's going to be a happy fucking kid
and
I'll be a happy fucking father
just
ignoring the fact that we will be dead in 20 years
from all the shit
humanity did to this poor planet...

he will know the truth one day
and
I might be gone by then
but
for now
for fucking now
he's going to have a great time and live a
comfortable life

until then...

the dread

of waking up alone
in that lonely hotel room
while on vacation alone
after an amazing night of getting fucking
hammered
totally fucked up
by yourself
all night
trying to talk to strangers
running away from your life at home
thinking this is so much more fun
because you can do whatever you want
at any time
hoping to meet some hot cool drunk chick
to go back to the room with
and
now
you are here
alone
fucking
alone
in this hotel room
far away from home
sick as a dog
and the thought of last night
makes you want to puke more
because it was so desperate and you
wish you could just be back in your
own bed
with your dog
in your normal life
but
you are here and you need to go back out
for another day
and there's not enough alcohol in Vegas to

transport you back 20 years to when
this was cool…and not totally depressing and
lame as hell…

the fun job

how the hell do these people do it?

yeah
great
it's some stupid fun job
and
they feel good going in everyday
and
totally fulfilled
but
it's not going to last!
(is all I think seeing them on TV)
how can it?
going around
to restaurants and eating food around the city
or
standing in front of a traffic report or a weather
map
looking hot
smiling
so happy they aren't at some shit job

but
it never lasts…it never does…
but they don't seem to care…

maybe they do

and they are just great actors…

poor bastards…

40 years old

just hit a squirrel

fucker ran out
too fast
and
I'm good at braking for those
coke addict fuckers

but
there was nothing I could do…

and
I felt more bad for that dumb
tree rat
than
I do the poor people in the war
in Ukraine
and that makes no sense
but
makes total sense
in that it was right in front of me
and I will never
meet those people who will die soon
and it's not just me
because we over here
in this great country
keep living our lives
like nothing is happening…what insane
logic…but we are people…we don't know
anything…

it's automatic at this point
I've seen him 3 times today
and
I always wave

my neighbor
a white guy
same age as me
kinda looks like me
and
we are both locked up
in middle age
doing the same shit in our nice houses
with our wives and kids
and
we are so close
if we were 10 years old
we would be best friends
but
nope
we get together with our wives
a few times a year
and we drink beer
and talk football and jobs
and
life
and then
we won't see each other for months
even though
we are so close
just next door………………………fucking marriage……..fucking
work………………no wonder men
can't get past high school…………thank fucking god though….

who needs more friends?

not me.

maybe a few more years

they all got together
after so many years
maybe 20?
and
seeing these pictures
these people are all melting
they look horrible
sorry to say
but
they do and it's hard to watch...

yes
they are younger than me and they look like they are in their
50's
what the fuck are they eating!!!!!

I might be there soon
but
for now
I'm holding it down

keep eating carrots
keep running
keep drinking beer
keep jerking off
keep fucking my wife
keep drinking water
keep working
keep listening to bad music
keep doing pull ups
keep painting
keep writing

and
maybe

you will make it
longer than you thought...

a place far away

watching the horse race
the small clip
that went viral
the horse and the jockey both
went down
violently
and it was horrible to see
and all I could care about was if the horse
was ok
that poor beautiful beast
I could give a fuck about that stupid
midget man riding on him
and
I'm not alone
we all love animals more than people
which makes no
fucking sense
does it?
we ALL HATE PEOPLE! WHY? WHY?
WE HATE ALL OF THEM!
and
we love animals!
even the evil fuckers
like snakes and spiders
they are scary but they should live
somewhere far away…right…

finally all alone

it's been so long
so
what do I do?

call a friend to hang out?

no

I spend it alone

this time is precious
why
fuck it up
with another person
and their problems?

alone
I can do whatever I want
and
I know it's sad
but
I don't care

life is short
I need to do what I want to do
and
they don't tell you that as a kid.

just log on

and
you see a million people
on
perpetual vacation
nobody is working
nobody
nobody
holy fucking shit
nobody is working!
how the hell do we
do anything? how is shit fixed
how does this country run?
everyone is on the beach
doing stupid shit!
how do they keep it up?
without going broke?
I don't know
I will never know
I will keep working until I die
and
they
they
will do a day of work and live like
kings…

get away

I finally had it! cut them all out of my life!
all they do is bring you down
fuck em!
feels great! I wish I did this years ago!

they say
now they are on top:

successful,
making tons of money,
have a good looking spouse,
kids,
big house,
isolated from everything and everyone

NO SHIT! what the hell kind of advice is
that?

when you got nothing
and
are making your bones in this world
you gotta rely on stupid fucks
to get by
you have to deal with the bullshit of those
assholes
who want to shit all over everything you do
because
you are poor and lonely and depressed
and have nothing else except
the hope that one day
you can get away from them
forever

which
the lucky ones

have done

and
now hearing this stupid advice

I want to scream

WITHOUT THOSE NEGATIVE IDIOTS
DRIVING YOU TO WORK AND WORK AND
WORK EVERYDAY IT'S LIKELY
YOU WOULD HAVE NEVER MADE IT AS FAR
AS YOU DID!

but who the fuck knows. I don't know anything.

I'm just a hungover fool at a old keyboard.

Greg Rivard

we all had that kid in our class
that one kid
who was severely handicapped
that poor unlucky child
who could barely function
in school

the one I'm talking about in my life
was named

Greg Rivard.

I'll never forget his name. he was like the character
Timmy in South Park.

but it wasn't funny like that. even then
in 3rd grade or 4th grade or whenever it was
I really have no idea how long he lasted

maybe 1st – 4th grade?

all I know is
we all felt super sorry for him
and
nobody made fun of him

that's how bad he was

in that wheel chair
slow talk
head bobbing around

God just thinking about it now
and
now having a child of my own

I want to cry

cry like a baby

it's not fucking fair

and then I clearly remember his mom always around
there
helping him

and it was totally normal for us because we all knew
God had fucked him good.

I have no idea what his diagnosis was. who the fuck knows.
probably
many things all together.

but
then
we come back from summer break
maybe
5th grade or 6th
and he's gone. he disappeared. and I didn't realize it then
no
only now
did I realize he was just gone. nobody talked about him
or said a word
but
he was gone
and
we went along with our lives like he never existed.

maybe he died or his parents decided to keep him home
because he got worse physically?

who fucking knows. all I can see in my mind is him
trying to talk

and it's all slow and I feel so bad and his mom
with her glasses and weird haircut with those dead eyes

and I can't imagine having to deal with that...fuck!

driving home

almost there
2 more minutes
and
then
you come to a huge line of cars…on a usually
empty back road…fucking hell…must be some kind of
construction..

you are pissed but it's whatever…another 5 minutes you will past
it…
seems to be moving along…and then
at the front
you see
it's some poor damn guy
peddling along
this road
going up hill

old guy too
really using all his strength
to
get where he's going

and

you immediately
feel bad for him
but

there's no way you can help him
you will never offer him a ride
no
no
no
fuck no

fuck no no no
he's probably nuts
so
you just
drive by
and then
you write this poem
for him
and then go to bed…that's all you can do…

we see too much

with all this damn technology
we see all the horrors of the world
and now
everyday we wake up
we think
it's going to end today
so
what's the point?
so
let's just get drunk and high and
eat
anything we want

SPEND AWAY!

retirement is a stupid god damn lie!

we will never make it! the bombs will be dropped
well before we turn
70!

so let's get fucked up! now is all that matters!

maybe it's for the best…we have to much
are too sad
shit needs to go back to the way it used to be
when
we wiped our asses with leaves and
were just happy to be alive
and have any kind of food

now
we invent problems because we have it
so good
but

that's what we do

we can't reprogram ourselves

all I know is
I don't want to be around for the end

I was born into this kind of
American life

modern American life
and it's so fucking awesome

I don't want to live any other kind of existence

no
no
no
I can't handle it…I'll happily dead
before I live in the forest eating bugs…

FOMO NOMO

being able to see all the craziness of the world
all the fun
people are having on social media
constantly traveling and partying and doing
crazy stupid shit
I have no jealous bone in my body
it all looks exhausting
at this point
but
I am happy to see it, to be entertained by it, to
experience a little bit of it
by just turning on my phone and opening an app
seeing these pretty people who would never have
anything to do with me anyway
so
it kind of works out like this…but if it was 20 years prior
and I was single and alone in my house
and had that desire to go out and have as much fun as possible
with hot girls…and couldn't…I might have literally killed myself
because that feeling and desire to be apart of something
was greater than anything else in the world at that time…but
now?
now I feel like a superhero. you can't hurt me with your videos
of getting drunk with thousands of hot girls on spring break.

driving by

he sits out there
in his wheel chair

I only see him
on Wednesday's and Friday's
when I pick up my son
from his grandmother's house

fuck…is all I think as I drive by this person…I have no idea how
old this guy
is…
a kid or grown adult is waving at me
and the rest of traffic
behind and in front of me…the parents just wheel him
out and he's seems so happy seeing cars and I'm so fucking
depressed at how mentally handicapped his is
and am so glad that's not my son…that was all I thought about
before he was born…having a kid like that…
I thought I was doomed…all the drinking and the stupid
shit…God was
going to fuck me…but so far so good…

these fucking stoners

they got it made
puffing away all god damn day
from morning to night
and they are totally fine going through life
like us all but
they are high as shit
and it doesn't faze them!

how great is that!

imagine being drunk
all day
and being able to go to work and
get everything done you need to get done
but
nothing really affects you because you are so fucked up

but
it's not like that with us drunks…pot…it doesn't fit with us…
our brains our different. we want to smoke to save our lives
to give us another 20 years of life
but
when we puff away
we get paranoid and we feel like shit
time goes so slow
get tired
feeling our whole body feeling like were dying…

the best I can explain it…it's like putting a triangle piece
into a square hole
you can hammer it in
and it will fit
but the whole time
it feels like shit

but
that drink...it's a square...it fits right in
and
after a few
you know it's the right fit....yup....gonna die young but fuck it
it feels so good......so right.....

they keep us going

we're so obsessed with lunatics…all of them

the rapists
the murderers
the cheaters
the sociopaths
the psychopaths
the frauds
the drunks
the drug addicts
the thieves
the scoundrels
and all the others I'm forgetting…

we go to work and we try and live as
normal lives as possible
and all the while
we read and watch about these crazy people
(fictional and non)
all day long…

it's what gets us by…it's what keep us entertained…
keeps us from going out of our minds
from the sheer boredom of the living
"The American Dream"
staying in that straight line

it keeps us waking up every day and going to work
so we can pop on some dumb show on our lunch break
about some maniac husband who poisons his wife
with antifreeze so he can cash out her life insurance and
marry his mistress…

people are the same all over

all you do is say you have to get away from
these nutjobs
these fucking crazy fuckers
and
then
one day
you show up at a new place to work
and
think it's going to be different, think it's going to
be *better*
and then
within a few days
you realize
they are just as insane as the last batch of
fuckwads
and
then you know why you keep your mouth shut and
avoid all eye contact
and
pretend to be invisible as much as possible
because
it's the only way to not assimilate into
their bullshit.

we don't do shit

we listen to these seasoned comics
who have been working at this shit for 10 plus years
on the road
playing every city in the country
from stupid dive bars and fire halls to arenas
the

we listen to these seasoned comics
who have been working at this shit for 10 plus years
on the road
playing every city in the country
from stupid dive bars and fire halls to arenas
they make it look so easy
just talking on stage like a normal person
with no fear

we all think we can do it
we can get up there
and speak our truth and talk about our lives
and make thousands of people laugh
with our observations of what is going in the world

and
it's a ridiculous fantasy
much like
when we put ourselves on stage in a famous rock band
when we are in high school

it's all so fucking stupid and yet
we think we can do it…we can't do shit except work our
dumb jobs and eat and drink and watch TV. that's all we are good
for
and
paying taxes and fucking and making more average people

who won't ever do anything special...yes that's
what we do
we
don't do shit...

and the only thing that can pull us out of this
imaginary existence is seeing some horrible open
mic-er get up there and totally bomb and it's all quiet
in the audience and he's talking about shit you were thinking
about
joking about
and
then
you are happy you have a good job and never even tried to do
anything
besides work and buy shit...

I saw them

these guys with the shaved heads
and the tattoos and the muscles
who weren't afraid of and saw them

these guys with the shaved heads
and the tattoos and the muscles
who weren't afraid of anything (seemingly)
who broke the rules without even thinking if it was bad or good
who drank and did drugs
who had other cool and dangerous friends and the girls loved
them

fuck! I thought! all I wanted to be was like them!

how though?

I didn't have one bad bone in my body!

how about this…I tried to shave my head and get tattoos and act
tough and break the rules

that's all it will take…

and it obviously didn't work…nobody believed it
nobody cared, nobody wanted anything to do with me

because

I don't have a bad bone in my body
I'm not that way

I'm quiet and boring and dumb and
just a regular joe
who just wants to be left alone

and that is what has saved me from
all the dangers of the world
so far

because
now
all those guys I looked up to
all those maniacs
who were constantly getting tons of chicks
who were smoking cigarettes
who were cool without even thinking about it

they are in the gutter or dead

nothing panned out with them. they burned out
like rock stars who never made it

way too fast...and here I am
being who I am

a nobody who is finally left alone
in my room , sipping on coffee
early in the morning
in a nice big house
in anytown USA
married to a good woman (who like me has no
bad bone in her body)
sleeping in the bedroom with
my 2 year old son
and
nothing could be better.

us humans

god what a disease we are on this earth
like a horrible virus!

we have slaughtered so many fucking elephants
they now have evolved to not
grow ivory tusks!

good for them!

but
do you think we will stop killing them?

NO!

NO!

NO FUCKING WAY ON EARTH!

we will still blow their brains out so some asshole
can chop off it's head and mount it on a wall
above the fireplace in their mansion…

FUCK THEM ALL! FUCK US ALL!

sometimes…

sitting here at 41
feeling over the hill
looking down and happy
the fight is over
no more climbing the mountain
I didn't get as far as I thought
as a child and then as a teen and
later in my 20's
but
who cares at this point? I'm still alive
and life is comfortable and I'm still at the keyboard
after 5 years which means
I might be at this for the rest of the time I'm alive
on this pointless planet
and
that's all I can ask for. almost everything else
in life
gets thrown in the garbage the day after you die
but
writing…sometimes writing lives on. sometimes. not always.
and
even though nobody will ever read this when I'm alive
it sometimes gets some attention
when
people kick the bucket and you can't talk to them
anymore…

sometimes…

out here

on my way home from work
at the traffic light
on a busy road
in the suburbs
I look over to the right and there was a hobbit man
long red hair
big beard
big and fat in a tye dye shirt
eating a burrito

this site in the city
would be nothing

just another nut job among the other
million lunatics running around

but out here

it's something else. he stands out. he's lonely.

he's alone. nobody walks around here like that
and
there he is. given up on life.

ALONE. it's so depressing seeing people like that out here.

they don't belong here. they need to get to the city. they fit
in there. you can be as fat as you want, smoke as much as you
want
eat as much as you want, dress like a vagrant…people don't care!
you
blend in…but out here?

not so much.

nice trick

to get away with some stupid or
bad behavior that you exhibit
around your woman or man you are
fucking

all you have to say to your spouse is

"I'm sorry, I'm such a mess!"

and then
will immediately feel bad for you
and
won't care that you have been acting
insane lately

it's just that easy.

they showed a picture of the guy
a 20 something man
said he was jewish and he had a tattoo of a jewish
star
on his chest
and
the white supremisist didn't like that
so
th guy
a 20 something man
said he was jewish and he had a tattoo of a jewish
star
on his chest
and
the white supremisist didn't like that
so
they beat the poor kid to death…
and
I was sad to hear that
but
I wasn't that sad…it was just another death of a person
I never met…another….and another…it seemed
the murder was never going to end
and
then
I scrolled down
and
it shared his story

he was a nice kid
and
he got hooked into heroin
in high school
and
that was it

that was it
that was it

it's the end

he bought drugs from the wrong guy
and
then arrested
and
in jail
and then they fucking kill him

the poor guy…

and they show a picture of him
on a lawn tractor
as a 3 or 4 year old with his dad
and
it melts me
it fucks me up
for days…weeks

how the hell? no…eli will never….he's my baby boy
my perfect baby boy…smiling baby boy…I won't ever let
anything happen…

holy trinity

this new author
just read his first book from 1951
a pool hustler book
and
ran through it easily in less than a week
after trying to
get through the first 10 pages of
at least 20 books before
and thinking
I had lost it, I couldn't read, I was now
illiterate and dumb
finally my phone and the internet and TV
took my brain
but
god damn I still got it and
when I looked the guy up
it said he was a degenerate who liked three things:

drinking
gambling
smoking

and
it made total sense why I could connect with his writing
and
now I'm on his 2nd book
about the Martian who fell to earth who
became a total alcoholic because of course
it makes total sense you live on this planet long enough
it gets to you and you need something to get by
on a daily basis
and all I think is
this guy gets it.

herd immunity

wait…not yet…one more minute…

you want to leave now but you can't. just fucking
wait. it will be worth it…

and then a minute goes by…

ok, now it's ok. you can trudge to the time clock
everyone will be cleared out
a minute earlier though…it would be a giant line
of people
but now
it's ok…

you've timed this perfectly. took a few times but
you now know when to leave to avoid everyone.

and then
you go down the hall and it's empty and perfect
you hit that time clock and head towards the double doors

then outside
you see the cattle herd of union humps
such as yourself
trudging towards that pointless temporary
freedom

thinking
this is it! almost there.

but all you are focused on is one man

a jolly man
a very nice man

a talkative man

you have nothing against this man. he's one of the good ones. but
you just want to walk in silence. you have nothing to say to
everyone.

and that's ok.

you walk fast because that's all you can do. you tried to walk slow
but
you can't.

so soon
you see the man
only 10 feet away. but he's chatting up three other men
and
you feel good. this is good. you might catch up
and be very close
soon
but
he won't see you. he's involved with those suckers.

and then
you go through the turnstiles
and
here it is
the moment of truth…where everyone seperates.

some go towards the parking garage
some
to the parking lot

and
this is where
he always gets you
that last walk to your car
when

everyone he was talking to
goes to the parking lot
while
we go to the garage.

but there's three this time. good odds. you are feeling good.

then
one guy with a backwards hat peels off. goes to the lot.

ok, two.
then
up the stairs
and
then
they say goodbye for 5 seconds while you approach
and
your chest tightens…he's going to spot you!

the third man keeps walking to the right where the
happy man parks his car
and
a second later
he see's the third man
and runs up and attaches himself like a virus
all while you
are 5 feet away
behind
with herd immunity
thanks to others being infected
and the man has no idea you were there the whole time

you feel a relief
like never before. it would have only been a 10 second
small talk chat and it seems ridiculous
at how much thought and energy is put into
avoiding it

but
you love the game. the avoiding game.

you are a master
it's your whole being

some people are really good at their jobs or karate or
cooking or making money

you
you will always be good at
avoiding people without them knowing
you are avoiding them

and that
is a damn fine skill to have in this world

it keeps you safe from all the monsters and non-monsters
 in this world

keeps as much of your time to yourself

and that's more important that money.

sit back and relax

these aging famous fuck
comedians
sitting on big piles of money
haven't created anything somewhat
funny
in
20 years
because they don't have to
it's too fucking hard
and I don't blame them for being lazy and
doing bad movies and cartoons where they
show up and read some lines and
put on a voice and pretend to be excited
like they were
early in their career when they wanted to
conquer the world…

no I don't blame them
sit back
and relax if you can

let the old shit
be the old shit
we remember
don't try and put out some
average material

because that is all it will be,
the anger and energy of youth is gone
so
just live the good life
like you are doing
stay
obscure for most of your life and
come out of your hole every few years

to
cash an easy check for some
role you don't even know what
it's about
written by some
hack Harvard grad
trying to make it like you did...so many years ago.

smacked down

I stood in line
at the liquor store
the day before
memorial day
with all the party people
in summer clothes on a hot day
all them loading up on as much booze as they
could carry
and in front of me
was a very good looking
in shape man
with cool tattoos
the kind of guy you look at in high school and go

I want to be like him, he probably gets tons of chicks

and I see his teenage son standing next to him. he's big and bulgy
with a bad haircut
and is dressed awfully
probably like I would have looked back then

but the dad is looks like he loves him
the kid might have some kind of disorder because when
they go up to the counter he has to kind of lead him up there
and
I feel kind of better about the world
because this guy
who probably crushed pussy and everything in life
is now
having to face reality
that
not everything about him is cool as shit anymore
he got smacked down with this
video game playing nerd of a son
and

he loves him to death and I feel better if
my son
is a big nerd
which is entirely possible
because I'm his father and we all know the apple falling from the
tree bit.

season 2

you see there is another season of that
surprising original show you watched
last year
burned through that shit in 2 days because it was so
fucking good
and
then
you turn it on
episode one
and
after a half an hour
you look over at your spouse and go

"what the hell is going on here?"

"I have no idea"

"this sucks"

and then you decide to turn it off watch some dumb
reality show

and all I'm thinking is

these stupid fucks
if you don't have a good idea for a second season
then
DON'T MAKE IT! IT'S OK!
you got lucky with a good premise and everything worked
because you didn't think the show would work
but then it turned out to be great and people liked it
but you panicked and came up with some bullshit
on the fly and now you have left a bad taste in my mouth
with this show
but really

it doesn't matter
it's not like I'll ever watch the first season again
for some reason
they don't make television shows for rewatching
over and over like back in the day
it's all one and done and a month later I'll never remember
anything about it.

my people

perusing through the DVD's at the thrift store
the old woman is in the way
I see
Match Point there
and want to grab it and go back to work to watch it
and I try and be patient but she's not moving
so
I just ask her to move so I can
get it.

then I keep looking and she shows me a copy of The Matrix
she's holding

"did they make a sequel to this?"
she asks.

"yeah, two actually. but they suck. just watch the original," I
say.

and she goes

"maybe I'll try to find the box set."

what a fucking weirdo
I think
and
then I think
no
you are a weirdo too. what are you doing looking for
DVD's on your lunch break at the thrift store
when you make 100k now
but
this is what my life is and I'll never change
so
fuck it all!

sizzle

the new thing in Hollywood
is taking documentaries and making them
scripted dramas
and
it's fantastic. we love seeing A-list actors
take over the lives of these
nutjobs who they
make these doc's about. but they put a spin
on them
and make up some shit to add some
spice and sizzle and
the real people are bitching that it's not the truth
but
nobody cares if it's real or not. we just want to be
entertained. it's fucking fun! you can yell as loud and
long as you want
nobody cares. nobody wants the truth. the truth is
boring. we want to be dazzled
what ever gets the blood flowing!
and
really…it doesn't matter. in a month the show will
be over and everyone will forget
because they will be onto the new thing and
in a fucking year if you ask me about the show
I won't know anything about it. I won't remember.

and then

those first few cords of the bass line
come on
and then I'm transported back to my dorm room
freshman year
watching comedy central at 2pm
but now I'm watching myself watching
The Kids in the Hall
alone
between classes
thinking
this is the most amazing show I've ever seen
what the fuck is this shit?

and day after day after day
I'm insanely entertained
and taken out of my horrible life
as an 18 year old virgin
horribly depressed thinking
I'm never going to get laid

and then
I text Lomack

we're both 41 and it's Friday night and we're both
drunk

dude, no more of this 2 year bullshit
we can hang once a year, it's one fucking day!

he agrees. he's going to come down in a month.

and it feels good. we're going to die
maybe soon
maybe later
but

we have to relive the past
as much as we can
because
when it comes down to the end
we will regret
not getting together and getting hammered
more

and that's the god damn truth.

breaking out of jail

I stare out the window
at 9am
with my coffee
the neighbor is mowing his lawn
and
I'm jealous. he's going to have a nicely cut lawn
by 11am
and he will be done for the day. I would go out there now and
get mine done
but
my family loves me and wants to be around me
all the time
and
I love them
but
getting out there on that mower
popping in some ear buds and listening to a podcast
on a nice
nice
nice
fucking day
smelling the fresh cut grass
not being bothered by anybody
is
really
really
really
nice.

at the end

another day
no reading
and
I feel bad
but
then
I think…at the end of my life
will I think

I wish I read more fucking books…

no
no
no

that won't come into my brain at all…

now writing…yes, I will think I didn't fuck around
at work
watching dumb shit
instead of writing stories…

but reading?

no
no
no

you can have it. I've read enough. and that's going to
be my bad karma as nobody will ever read anything I've
written and I've made peace with that. I'm like a shitty Kafka
but I don't have the balls to tell my family to burn my shit when
I
die.

(and yes, I know that reading does help writing but it's very time consuming and I still love it when I get a good one)

it's been a while

finally a good one
a nice, happy, young girl who seems to love her job
she smiles and is very peppy and
asks about my day as she takes my information about the
package
that I'm sending out
I tell her it's a computer for my wife's old job and the peppy and
asks about my day as she takes my information about the
package
that I'm sending out
I tell her it's a computer for my wife's old job and they need it
back
and she asks about her and says she's happy
my wife has a new job and tells me to tell her good luck with it
and then I pay and she hands over the receipt in that horizontal
way
like she's handing me a baby and still smiling smiling smiling
and
I tell her to have a great fucking day and she says the same
but we both don't say the f word but it sounded better
in this poem
and I leave andys the same
but we both don't say the f word but it sounded better
in this poem
and I leave and feel really good about the world for a few seconds
actually seeing some kid
who is happy to have a job…

they finally got me

the bastards
the TV fucks
every company with their own
streaming service
I used to tell myself I wouldn't get sucked in
I would only subscribe to one or two and the
rest can go fuck themselves
I'll find the shit for free somewhere if they come out with a
show I want to watch or I'll do a month free trial and then
cancel after watching that one show that looked good…

and now

I'm paying at least 5 streaming services…

maybe more?

I don't know. I don't care anymore. they beat me. I can't keep
trying to play the games

they have what I want and like an addict
I pay them for my drugs and I'm happy and I don't
care about the money anymore.

take it. between 50 and 100 a month for the streaming
and
another 200-250 for cable.

take it.

let me hook this shit up to my veins
and
I'm happy. in blissful ignorance and not thinking
about how the world is collapsing

on my comfy couch…with the wife and child
in the big house
in this nice neighborhood

away from it all…

nod and smile and agree

nothing better than
listening to someone who is so invested in politics
explaining how their side is the *right* side
how the other side is ruining the country and
we have to vote those fuckers out in November
and
you just nod and agree and laugh
not caring either way
just amazed
how they think about this shit all day and they are
DEAD SERIOUS
as they talk passionately about
how we need to take this country back
from the evil fuckers
and
all I am thinking is
about how
the corrupt political machine
this American government that has fooled us
that we are living in a democracy
and
how the whole thing is fixed
like some god damn 80's wrestling fight
where both guys beat the shit out of each other
and it's bloody and it looks so fucking real
and
then one guy gets pinned and half the country cheers
and half the country is angry
and
then after the show the two guys
drinking beers together
as they count their money
laughing at the stupid crowd
knowing they pulled another fast one on
all of us.

again here

thinking about the past
and everything I never did
and
not caring at all
all those places in the world
people talk about visiting
and how amazing it was and how
they have many more places to visit
things to see
people to meet...

I grew up in a suburb of Philadelphia
went to college an hour away
in the middle of the state
then
came back and moved 5 minutes away from where
I grew up...

got a job 19 minutes away...

got married a few years later...

went on vacation a few times
once
overseas for the honeymoon
and then a cruise
and then
keywest...

then moved to a house 20 minutes away from where
I grew up...

then got divorced and remarried...

and now I still live 20 minutes away from where I grew up...

with the child and new wife and some dogs
and have no desire to go anywhere...

and that's enough for me...

the rest of the world can do what it does without my footprint...

I'll die without ever seeing any of it
in person...

it doesn't matter...

no one will ever care

nothing sadder than a poor old man
who gave his life to some creative
pursuit

and never made it.

he's almost dead now
living in some awful existence

alone and angry

never having made any kind of fruitful life

and he's there in that little apartment
in some unknown city
probably drunk
still hoping this next line will give him his

b
i
g

break.

some point

I hate all these poems
I agree with the rest of the world
it's all very stupid and silly waste of time
but
one good thing that keeps me going
keeps me typing like a lunatic
is
when I'm bored
when I have 15 minutes to myself
in my office
I'll pull off an old collection from my shelf
something I wrote at least 5 years prior
and I'll page through and read some of it and
it's interesting to see where I was in the world at that time
in my life
at that younger age
usually I'm angrier and more depressed than I am in the present
and that makes me kind of happy
knowing I'm making some sort of progress
in this pointless existence
and
it keeps me writing
like I am right now
with the coffee
while the baby and woman are asleep
at 5:48am.

and again

you step out into the summer night

(I've written this a million times...)

and the hot air hits you
not so hot
but
just right
and

you have a few drinks in you
and
all you want to do is light up a butt
and
sit on your 10,000 deck...but you are 41 and have a
2 year old
and you want to live until he graduates high school
so
you go back in the air conditioning
and
try and not think about it...

the main men

sitting here
almost drunk
waiting for the click
like Paul Newman in
Cat on a Hot Tin Roof
writing poems
feeling good with my hands on the keys
and
all I can think about is how
Faulk
wrote all those god damn amazingly
complicated books
totally fucked up…he doesn't get his due

like the 86 Mets…all those guys
fucked up on drugs and booze

they won it all… and you gotta respect that…

being able to rise above us normal
idiots

and
doing not in the right mind

but
then

maybe that helped them…maybe that was their right mind…

gave them the strength and courage
to squash all doubt…being totally fucked up….

YES!

YES!

and as I write this I realize…the click just came
and

NO ONE CAN TELL ME SHIT!

I CAN WRITE WHATEVER I WANT!

SO LET'S GO MOTHERFUCKER!

insulated

here in my house
in the suburbs
my whole life
things have been easy and painless
and
boring
which is the way I like things
I'm happy without any drama or excitement
just calm
calm
calm
calm
that's all I can ask for
it's no wonder I am drawn the sedative nature of
booze
just
put me to sleep
slowly
without a fight and I'll be happy.

this is now and that was then

looking at her picture
after 5 maybe 6 years not seeing her...

damn fucking strange

we were married for 10 years?

how is that possible?

who is that person?

she's pretty much a doctor now
and
back then

she was so sick she couldn't work...

who is this person?

to forget

the money is there
and
life is good
so
                                          it's so easy to forget
about how
the world is totally fucked..

just keep having kids and spending boat loads of dollars on
stupid bullshit

it's how we forget…
damn shame

coming up on 3 years since I've been to the city.

fucking war zone now.

damn shame.

 I miss the urine soaked shithole.

if I was single I wouldn't care.

but now I have to take calculated risks.

too much to lose.

damn shame.

I haven't seen a comedy show in a long time.

people are getting mowed down and robbed and beaten
at all hours of the day.

even in the nice parts of the city.

and no one is safe.

damn shame.

no matter

another collection of poems
to add to the shelf above
my computer
and
again I'm amazed at how many I'm up to now
somewhere in the 10-20 range
closer to 20…I could count but I really don't care
anymore. it's just words. unedited bullshit words.
and I always think it's going to be my last
thing I put out
because coming up with another couple of hundred poems
seems impossible
and a waste of time…but then after a few months…they are there
again
all in line, ready to go…and I don't remember writing
any of them,
no matter if I write them in the early morning or
late at night.

I can die now

it was the best day ever
today
started off
sleeping in
and was greeted by the wife and child and
watched some TV and then
had a hearty breakfast of
sausage, eggs, cheese and a white toasted muffin
with butter (turned into a sandwich)
and then
we went for a walk, it was January 2nd but
wasn't very cold (which is probably going to
be bad for us in a few or a hundred years)
and then
the woman went to the gym
and
I put the kid in for a nap
while I went on the computer and played an old
dos game (kind of like Dungeon and Dragons) instead
of running
because I had to enjoy the bit of time I had in the house
alone and then I looked at my fantasy football line up
and made sure it was good to go (for the first time ever, I was in
the championship game, where the winner got 800 bucks) and
then
set my normal football bets
and then
the woman came home around an hour later
and we both showered and then we fucked
really good
because the kid was still sleeping
and then
we dressed and got ready to go out to the coffee shop
where we met
5 years prior

and then the parents came over and released us from
responsibility
and then we drove down and got our coffee and sat
in those same seats we sat
not knowing at the time we were looking at our future
soulmates
and then
we took pictures and smiled to commemorate the moment
(if I was younger I would have never done this, I would have
thought
it was stupid and I was too cool to do that shit but now I realize it
doesn't
matter and who gives a fuck what other people think)
we went and hit the bar across the street, another
one of our places that we frequented
in our younger years
and as we walked in
I saw they had two giant tv's, both showing football
and
a calm came over me
this is going to be an amazing afternoon I thought
and then
we sat at the almost empty bar
ordered drinks
and we talked and talked
not looking at our phones
about the past and everything that we had been through
all the wonderful things
that happened in the short time since we met
all the while
the football games were going on in the background
and every few minutes I checked my team and my points kept
going up and up and up…
holy shit, I could win this thing! I thought.
so then we finish up our early dinner and drive home and
the baby comes running in to see us with a big smile on his face
and the dogs are so happy to see us and

my parents are there and everyone is smiling
I look at my phone and see that I am blowing away my fantasy
football opponent by at least 100 points. the Cincinnati Bengals
had an all time game against the Kansas City Chiefs and my three
guys

Joe Burrow
Jamar Chase
Joe Mixon

all put up insane numbers to give me my first championship win
ever
which
yes
seems like something a child would be happy about
and
I admit I am a child but I don't care. my wife can't believe I won
800 smackers and I have no idea what I'm going to do with it

probably pay my credit card off.

because even though I act like a child I am an adult with
responsibilities.

then the parents leave and we settle in and watch some TV and
later the woman goes to bed and I get to watch more football and
I make even more money with the betting on my phone and I
think...

this year might be different...I've never had this much luck so
early on. maybe it's good, maybe it's bad.

well see.

J. Andrew Thomas was born in Hatfield, Pa where he attended Catholic school for 12 years before going to Kutztown University where he graduated in 2003 with a degree in biology. Soon after graduating he started working in the pharmaceutical industry and 12 years later he started writing fiction and poetry. He currently lives outside of Philadelphia with his wife and son.